# PARABLES
*Earthly Stories with a Heavenly Meaning*

# ANTHONY RITTHALER

# WALKING

## ON THE

# WATER

## WITH

# JESUS
### VOLUME TWO

## A BOOK OF HOPE
## PEACE, JOY, AND FAITH

PUBLISHED *by* PARABLES

*Earthly Stories with a Heavenly Meaning*

# ANTHONY RITTHALER

## Pathways To The Past

Each volume stands alone as an Individual Book
Each volume stands together with others
to enhance the value of your collection

Build your Personal, Pastoral or Church Library
Pathways To The Past contains an ever-expanding list of
Christendom's most influencial authors

Augustine of Hippo
Athanasius
E. M. Bounds
John Bunyan
Brother Lawrence
Jessie Penn-Lewis
Bernard of Clairvaux
Andrew Murray
Watchman Nee
Arthur W. Pink
Hannah Whitall Smith
R. A. Torrey
A. W. Tozer
Jean-Pierre de Caussade
Thomas Watson
And many, many more.

---

Title: Walking On The Water With Jesus (Volume 2)
Anthony Ritthaler
Rights: All Rights Reserved
ISBN 978-1-945698-01-9
Doctrinal theology, Inspiration
Salvation, Meditation
Other books by this author include: Walking On The Water With Jesus (Volume 1) and A Devil From The Beginning.

ANTHONY RITTHALER

# WALKING
## ON THE
# WATER
## WITH
# JESUS
### BOOK TWO

## A BOOK OF HOPE
## PEACE, JOY, AND FAITH

PUBLISHED *by* PARABLES

*Earthly Stories with a Heavenly Meaning*

# TABLE OF CONTENTS

# Special Thanks

I'm grateful in my heart for all the many people who contributed towards this project. So many prayed and offered help as I was putting this together. I am humbled by every act of kindness and every word of encouragement. I would like to give a special thank you to my friend and evangelist Todd Hicks and his wife for their donation without hesitation towards this effort for God. My friends, I believe God in heaven will reward you greatly for what you did. Also I would like to thank Miss Janine Burke and Kim White for their constant words of encouragement that refreshed my soul while writing. Thank you to my Godly parents who helped me every step of the way. Lastly I want to thank my lovely wife who helped me put this book together. Without her help this book would not be the same. I really appreciate everyone who helped make this happen.

With Love Bro Tony

# INTRODUCTION

Welcome to volume two of Walking on the Water with Jesus. Once again we will unfold some unbelievable blessings sent from the Throne Room of Heaven. Every story within the pages of this book are fresh and new and they will magnify our great Lord once again. The power of God flows through each unique story you will read, and you will be touched in many different ways. We will cover a vast array of blessings that are moving and encouraging in every sense of the word. I'm very confident that these stories are some of the best that you may ever hear during your lifetime. May Gods Spirit minister to our hearts in the pages to come, and show us that He can still do the impossible even today.

As I was writing these stories down, the Power of God was very evident within my soul. Although I will be the first to admit that my strength is small, I am glad to report "that I can do all things through Christ which strengtheth me." This entire book was written in sixteen hours, and God's Spirit helped me every step of the way. Your heart will be blessed for sure, and your faith will be enlarged for His glory. May we all look to God for the help we so desperately need and not towards feeble man. Without God we can do nothing and we should always remember that.

My goal, as always, is to give God the glory for the great things He hath done. If this book does not bless your heart in various ways; I will be the first to ask your forgiveness. In the pages to come I will do my best to lift up God in ways that are different, exciting, and glorious for the cause of Christ. My prayer is that this book will bring hope to the hopeless and peace to the down of heart. May God use this book for His honor and praise in the years to come.

Phillipians 4:13 "I can do all things through Christ which strengtheneth me."

# CHAPTER ONE
# GOD'S GOLDEN RULE

The precious word of God speaks much about the subject we will cover in this chapter. God has a way of rewarding those who show kindness throughout their days on earth. God the Father gives all mankind a free will to exercise the right to show pity and grace towards others, however it is up to us whether we obey His leadership or not.

Often in my life I have decided to help others and the response from God has been wonderful. Hebrews 6:10 says, "For God is not unrighteous to forget your work and labour of love, which ye have shewed toward his name, in that ye have ministered to the saints, and do minister." Almost every single day of my life people ask me about sowing and reaping and does it really work. Constantly I will respond by giving them real stories from my life; which proves that sowing and reaping really does work. Perhaps the most well known scripture in the bible is found in Galatians 6:7. Here the bible tells us that, "Whatsoever a man soweth, that shall he also reap." The bible plainly expresses to us that if we sow bad seeds in life trouble will spring up later on, but if we sow good seeds blessings will come our way. We as humans refuse to plant good seeds on a daily basis and that decision often plagues us over and over again. The more I determine to help others, the more God in heaven seems to help me.

Just a short while ago, God proved himself to me and a friend of mine that He still gives good gifts unto his children. According to Micah 5:2 he is from everlasting to everlasting and he is still in control. Please let me prove it to you.

While at work one afternoon I was talking to a man about the mercy of Christ. This man proceeded to ask me about this subject and he craved the blessings that were daily coming my way. I told him that the good Lord has allowed me to sow hundreds of precious seeds in my life and they are starting to come back for me. This gentleman then asked me if I had ever heard of the Golden Rule; which is simply do unto others that which would be done unto you. I quickly replied sure I have and even though it will never take you to heaven, it is a great rule to live by. We then talked much about God's blessings and the joy of helping others. We both enjoyed the conversation and God met with us that afternoon.

As work concluded, and I made it to my car, the Lord burned this subject in my mind, and I was reminded of the importance of encouraging others. It was after arriving at my home, later that day that I would discover the realness of the conversation that just transpired a little earlier. I remember asking my wife if we received any mail that day and she said we sure did. She handed me a check that arrived at 3:30 that afternoon and it was from the Golden Rule Company. It came at a time when we desperately needed it, and it was for $399.24. God seemed to manifest himself to us that day and prove his love in an amazing way. The Golden Rule Company overcharged us nearly four hundred dollars and we happened to get the reimbursement check on that exact day. Earlier in the day, as I was talking to the man from my work it was exactly 3:30 in the afternoon, and that is when the check made it to my mail box as well.

God always seems to send help when we need it the most. Trust in the Lord at all times, and start to sow good seeds along your journey and God will show up in your life. After all the Golden Rule has stood the test of time and so has God's Holy book. Do what's right and the Lord promises to bless you every time.

## *Scriptures Chapter 1*

Hebrews 6:10 "For God is not unrighteous to forget your work and labor of love, which ye have showed toward his name, in that ye have ministered to the saints, and do minister."

Galatians 6:7 "Be not deceived; God is not mocked: for whatsoever a man soweth, that shall he also reap."

Psalm 44:8 "In God we boast all the day long, and praise thy name forever. Selah."

Psalm 62:8 "Trust in him at all times; ye people, pour out your heart before him: God is a refuge for us. Selah."

# CHAPTER 2
# HOLDING OFF THE RAIN

We have a number of great stories contained within the covers of the Bible that blow our minds concerning our faith. According to Mark 4:39 we find that Jesus rebuked the wind and said peace be still and the wind ceased. Through Christ all things are possible and He proved it with the raging storm. It is through Christ that all things are possible, because He heard Joshua's prayer and made the sun stand still in heaven for a whole day. Joshua 10:14 declares that there was no day like that before or no day like it after that the Lord hearkened unto the voice of a man.

Through Christ all things were possible in the life of Elijah, who was a man just like you and I according to James 5:17. He had the power to shut off the rain for three and a half years and to turn it back on through the power of God. We limit God far too much and it is high time we start believing that He can do anything like His word teaches. So many today explain away His miracles and fail to believe they can happen today. Hebrews 13:8 says, "Jesus is the same yesterday, today, and forever." I can still remember, not long ago, when a young man asked me if God can still stop the rain like He did back then. I responded by saying to him, "Sure he can because he did it for me one day and I have witnesses." Let me tell a story that will bless your heart and prove Gods power once again.

A few years back, I remember waking up to reports that there was a ninety percent chance of rain for the day, and so I prepared myself for it. My heart sank because nothing is worse than having to work in the rain. At this point in my life, the hand of the Lord could be seen on a daily basis to those around me, and I knew He could do the unthinkable.

At around eight that morning a young lady approached me with a prayer request that tested my faith. Her exact words were, "We know you have power with God so can you hold off the rain today." My response to her was I'll see what I can do and I'll try to hold off the rain till five thirty. Dark clouds seemed to dwell over our yard but there was no rain coming. As the day wore on and five thirty approached the sky grew darker, but still not a rain drop fell from the sky. It was five twenty nine when I made it safe and sound into the building and a man said to me, "Well, I guess your prayers worked because no rain hit us." I still remember looking at him and saying, "I held it off till five thirty but I'm not responsible after that." Just as the words left my mouth, five thirty struck and we were pelted with heavy rain that made the building shake. For around twenty five minutes it rained cats and dogs outside but not before five thirty.

The Lord is very capable of displaying His wonders no matter what age we live in. Depend on His word above anything else, and allow Him to work in an awesome way. Hebrews 11:6 says, "That without faith it is impossible to please him."

## Scriptures Chapter 2

Mark 4:39 "And he arose, and rebuked the wind, and said unto the sea, Peace, be still. And the wind ceased, and there was a great calm."

Joshua 10:14 "And there was no day like that before it or after it, that the Lord hearkened unto the voice of a man: for the Lord fought for Israel."

James 5:17 "Elijah was a man subject to like passions as we are, and he prayed earnestly that it might not rain: and it rained not on the earth by the space of three years and six months."

Hebrews 13:8 "Jesus Christ the same yesterday, and today, and forever."

Hebrews 11:6 "But without Faith it is impossible to please him:"

# Chapter 3
# There is Rest in Christ

Sometimes, while on our journey through this life, we must take time to come apart and rest a while. God said in the Old Testament that on the seventh day He rested and He was refreshed. God knoweth the frame of man and He knows when enough is enough. Jesus told his disciples not to be overcharged with the cares of this life. The Lord also tells us to take all our burdens to the Lord and leave them there. According to the bible we must ordain certain times when we are to be wise about resting. Many of the great Christians that we read about and adore suffered premature health problems that could have been avoided if they would have rested more. When you are in the ministry and you love God it is hard to slow down and heed to the warning signals concerning your health. God has ordained rest for a reason, and He wants you to preserve your health so you can help more people for many more years.

According to statistics, the average preacher dies at around the age of forty five to fifty. The average life span of a person is seventy years of age and that is found in Psalm 90:10. There is sweet rest in Christ not just spiritually but also physically. Many good men and women die well before their time because they fail to get the proper rest they should. Statistics prove that a far greater percentage of people die due to stress rather than bad eating habits. The thing that is killing this country, in this generation, is uneasy spirits and stressed out people. I have had to train myself, over the years, to know when to say enough is enough, it is time to rest for a few days. In the remainder of this chapter I want to tell you story that will show you the goodness of God. It is a story that refreshes me whenever I tell it. I pray it will refresh you as well.

A few years back my batteries were very low and I was at the point of breaking down. My wife and I were raising our first child and I was working long hours, completing my first book, teaching, and many other little things. My wife and I sat down one day and discussed a possible vacation because it was long over do. Money was a definite issue at the time, but we had to do something. After talking it over I told my wife I would have to pray about the vacation and we would see what happens. The very next day we received a call from my sister-in-law with an answer to my prayer. They insisted that we go along with them to an indoor water park and they would pay our way. That week they paid for the room, food, Kabana, and many other things. It turned out to be a great week and the timing couldn't have been better. All in all they paid around one thousand two hundred dollars for us and refused to take any money. We will always remember there kindness till the day we die.

Always keep in mind, child of God, that when you serve the Lord he always offers rest when you need it most. Just listen to God when He offers sweet rest and you will be glad you did. Rest is a sweet thing and we can only bear so much child of God.

## *Scriptures Chapter 3*

Psalm 90:10 "The days of our years are threescore years and ten; and if by reason of strength they be fourscore years, yet is their strength labor and sorrow; for it is soon cut off, and we fly away."

1 Peter 5:7 "Casting all your care upon him; for he careth for you."

# Chapter 4
# Hearing a Sweet Voice
## on a Morning

One of my favorite songs growing up was the song Jesus is the Sweetest Name I Know. Its words seem to speak to me in a soft and moving way. This is also true concerning the voice of God. When He speaks, often it is in a sweet and lovely way that only His children can hear. Most of the time it is not loud and terrible, but rather tender and smooth as a morning dove. When His voice is heard, in our lives, it will grab our attention and it will give us peace in our hearts. There is nothing on earth like His gracious, eternal and life giving words that can stir the soul to no end.

When I think about His voice speaking to a heart, I think about the testimony of Gerald Crabb. By his own testimony, Mr. Crabb, who was a saved man, turned from the Lord and made a complete mess with his life. He let his family down, he lost his business and he failed the Lord through alcohol. He found himself working at a car wash and he only had the bottle to hold unto. One day as he was washing cars he said, from out of nowhere, he heard the sweetest voice he had ever heard and it was the Lord. Mr. Crabb said the Lord spoke to him and said I'm not done with you yet and if you will come back home I will forgive you of the mistakes you have made. Shortly after hearing God's voice, he began writing songs that are some of the best of this generation. God is a loving, patient, and forgiving God that treats us far better than we deserve. When His voice can be heard, sunrays of strength flood the soul and motivate us to do more for Him. For the rest of this chapter I will give you positive proof that He still speaks to hearts today.

On a Monday morning, as I was getting ready for work, I skipped breakfast as I was rushing out the door. I remember starting up the car and taking off to work. Before I left my housing complex, I realized I forgot my lunch. When I went to turn around that morning I suddenly heard the voice of God tell me to leave my lunch at home, because He would take care of me today. I followed the Lord's leadership and fully trusted that He would provide for me like He promised. I really didn't know how but I knew He would do something for me that day.

Later that day, at 11:20 a.m., a fellow co-worker approached me with some great news. He told me that Jimmie John Subs had provided us with around seventy five free subs to enjoy for that day. A sweet peace came over my soul because I knew that Christ provided for me like He said. What is even more incredible is the fact that all those subs were placed exactly in the area where I sit next to my bible. This story reminds me of young Samuel when he said, "Speak Lord for thy servant heareth." Praise the Lord.


## Scriptures Chapter 4

1 Samuel 3:10 "And the Lord came, and stood, and called as at other times, Samuel, Samuel. Then Samuel answered, Speak; for thy servant heareth."

1 Kings 19:12 "And after the earthquake a fire; but the Lord was not in the fire: and after the fire a still small voice."

# CHAPTER 5
# A SERVICE
# I WILL NEVER FORGET

There is a service that took place in a tent meeting, in Detroit Michigan, that still stands out in my mind. As I arrived there was excitement in the air, but before I left silence filled the church as God's judgment sweep through my soul.

Both preachers that night had wonderful reputations and are two of the very best men in this country. Both men preach in two completely different styles but both are powerful in their own unique way. One of these men preached like an Educated Isaiah and the other like a Fiery John the Baptist. One man has the biggest church in Michigan, and the other is possibly the greatest Evangelist in America. In other words, they are both anointed of God and are protected and sheltered by the Savior. Please permit me to give you a fatal story that should cause us to think twice before interrupting a service in a rude way when the Spirit of God is present.

As I arrived at the meeting that night joy rushed through my inner being, because of all the precious memories I had there through the years. Some of my fondest moments have taken place under that old tent, and the power of God is especially strong during those meetings. Some of the greatest preachers in the land mounted the pulpit that week and I was eager to hear from God. The good Lord has allowed me to pour much money into those meetings and it holds a special place in my heart.

When the service began that night everything seemed to flow well, and the singing seemed to be straight from Glory. After the song service concluded the first preacher was announced and he began his sermon. It seemed like the longer he preached the better it was. People's hearts seemed to be tuned into his message and we were receiving the Word with gladness. When the preacher arrived at the climax of his message something happened that swiftly changed the atmosphere of the night in a bad way.

From out of nowhere, as the preacher was speaking, the roaring of thunder rolled into the parking lot. The sound was so loud that it totally over took everything that the Man of God was saying. The sound had come from sixty tough, rugged bikers who wanted to make a grand entrance into Gods house. In my mind it was probably the rudest thing I had ever witnessed in my life.

It was exactly at that moment that I happened to make eye contact with the second preacher, who would speak that night, and we were both thinking the same thing. Proverbs 13:13 says "That whoso despiseth the word shall be destroyed." It seemed like God's spirit sweep over my soul and I knew God was going to judge that crowd for what they did. Sure enough as the second preacher mounted the pulpit, God's presence rested upon him for the next thirty minutes.

Near the end of his sermon, the preacher looked at me and said, "Bro Tony, someone is in trouble tonight and this will be their last chance to run to Christ." As it turned out no one accepted Christ that night as death was hovering over that tent. It was the very next day when we got a report that one of those bikers, who rudely distracted the gospel, was killed in a tragic way.

God has magnified His Word more than His own name; and when you laugh at it you will pay the ultimate price. A famous preacher has a message entitled Pay Day Someday. Be very careful how you treat the Lord, because no matter how tough you think you are, you are no match for Him. Always remember this verse "There is a way that seemeth right unto a man but the end thereof are the ways of death."

## Scriptures Chapter 5

Proverbs 13:13 "Whoso despiseth the word shall be destroyed: but he that feareth the commandment shall be rewarded."

Proverbs 14:12 "There is a way that seemeth right unto a man; but the end thereof are the ways of death."

Psalm 138:2 "I will worship towards thy holy temple, and praise thy name for thy loving-kindness and for thy truth: for thou hast magnified thy word above all thy name."

Isaiah 64:1 "Oh that thou wouldest rend the heavens, that thou wouldest come down, that the mountains might flow down at thy presence."

# CHAPTER 6
# MY GRACE
# IS SUFFICIENT FOR THEE

The apostle Paul said in II Corinthians 12:9, "God's grace is sufficient for thee: for my strength is made perfect in weakness." Paul dealt with pressures that we will never be able to comprehend, but he still was effective for Christ. Paul never seemed to walk in his own power, but always in the power of God. Life can get overwhelming at times but God's grace is a beautiful thing. Many of the greatest people of all time went through pain, lose of land, deaths, hardships, and trails, but God always helped them through it. God has never promised to remove storms from our life however he has promised to give us the grace to go through it. Often in the midst of our afflictions when we think it can't get any worse God arrives on the scene to offer relief. You will often find Gods grace with the death of a loved one. Jesus had compassion on Mary and Martha when there brother died and he does the same for you and me. The Lord will issue certain times in our life when he will send grace in many different forms and fashions. The word grace basically means unmerited favor, or Gods riches at Christ's expense. There have been many times in my life when the Lord has blessed me and sent things my way that I didn't have to work for. The story that I will now give proves Gods grace in my life and helps me to go another mile for Christ. The Lord is gracious and you will see it through this story.

One day as I was working in Detroit I noticed an unusual amount of churches with crosses on top of them. Nothing in this world means more to me then the cross of Jesus Christ. The great apostle Paul said it

23

best in Galatians 6:14 when he wrote, "God forbid that I glory save in the cross of Jesus Christ." At my home I have a cd about the cross that I have listened to around 80 times. There is divine power in the cross and it has changed this world like nothing else ever has. I would venture to say that while working in Detroit that day I seen around 60 crosses in 3 hours. As we were driving home that day I remember getting very low on energy and very thirsty. As we came closer to the shop that day I bowed my head and said a simple prayer asking the Lord for a candy bar and a Pepsi. When we made it back to the shop I immediately headed towards the break room to see if my prayer was answered. Sure enough as I entered the break room someone had put four little Hersey bars on my bible. What's even more amazing is the fact that whoever did this took the time to make it in the form of a cross. Instantly God seemed to invade my heart in a new way and I had to take a seat and ponder what just happened. Around 10 seconds later a Mexican man touched my shoulder and asked me if I wanted a Pepsi for free. God answered my prayer in a stunning way and this story helps me every time I tell it.

Let me close this chapter by saying whenever we hear stories like this it should really cause us to thank God for the grace that he sends our way. Without the grace of God our life would be empty and void. The old song writer had it right when he said nothing in my hand I bring but simply to the cross I cling.

## Scriptures Chapter 6

2 Corinthians 12:9 "And he said unto me, My grace is sufficient for thee: for my strength is made perfect in weakness. Most gladly therefore will I rather glory in my infirmities, that the power of Christ may rest upon me."

Galatians 6:14 "But God forbid that I should glory, save in the cross of our Lord Jesus Christ, by whom the world is crucified unto me, and I unto the world."

# Chapter 7
# A Sudden Change
# in the Air

No miracle that Jesus ever performed was quite like the day He calmed the Sea of Galilee. The storm was violent, the waves were crashing, and the disciples fear was very high. The whole area was on pins and needles and an uneasy feeling filled the air. The disciples on board truly felt like it was the end and they begged Jesus to do the impossible. What happened next shocked the world and proved the almighty power of God.

The Bible records that the Lord looked at the worst circumstance, known to man, and simply said, "Peace be still" and immediately there was a great calm. The birds started singing; the waves looked like a sheet of glass, and all stood in total amazement of what just transpired. This moment in time not only affected those on the ship, but also those on land.

According to Mark 5 we find that a man, who had six thousand demons, ran to Jesus and finally found peace in his soul when the Lord returned to shore. This man must have said to himself that if Christ can calm the raging sea, surely he can calm the storm in me. This calming of the sea prompted those disciples to make this statement "What manner of man is this that even the wind and the sea obey him?"

Throughout my time on earth I have often wondered if this was possible today. Can the Lord still do wonders in this day and age like he

...k then? Praise God I'm glad to report, with this following story, I have seen it with my own eyes. God is the God of the impossible and I'm thankful, in my soul, for this next story. Prepare to be amazed like we were that day and allow the Lord to minister to your heart with this story.

One Friday morning some of my coworkers and I got the call to pick up barrels on Woodward Ave. The sky looked pitch black, the atmosphere was gloomy and rain was most certainly coming our way. I was trying my best to keep our spirits up, but no one likes working in the rain and nothing seemed to help. What happened next still marvels me to this day.

As I was picking up barrels; the driver said to me that he hated working in weather like this and my response to him was swift and full of faith. I looked straight at him and said, "I will pray that God clears up the weather for us." To my amazement within thirty seconds every single dark cloud vanished from view and the sun was shining brightly upon us. Everyone's jaw dropped that morning and we had a wonderful day to work. The whole atmosphere changed and it felt like God was shining His light around us. The following Sunday I told this story at church and people's hearts were blessed.

We serve a supernatural God that can bring light to any situation, no matter how dark it may look. First John 1:7 says "but if we walk in the light, as he is in the light, we have fellowship one with another, and the blood of Jesus Christ his Son cleanseth us from all sin." What a joy to know that the Lord is always near and He is able to calm every storm that comes our way.

## Scriptures Chapter 7

Mark 5:6 "But when he saw Jesus afar off, he ran and worshipped him."

Mark 4:41 "And they feared exceedingly, and said one to another, What manner of man is this, that even the wind and the sea obey him?"

1 John 1:7 "But if we walk in the light, as he is in the light, we have fellowship one with another, and the blood of Jesus Christ his Son cleanseth us from all sin."

Matthew 21:22 "And all things, whatsoever ye shall ask in prayer, believing, ye shall receive."

# CHAPTER 8
# O TASTE AND SEE THAT THE LORD IS GOOD

People who have never encountered the grace of God can never fully understand just how wonderful Jesus really is. When you are an outsider looking in the cross seems bloody, sad, and cruel and you will never understand it. However when you are washed in the blood everything becomes bright, transparent, and new. The love of God has a way of changing mankind's outlook concerning heaven and hell and spiritual matters.

One of my favorite songs ever is the song "The Longer I serve him the sweeter he grows." One of my favorite verses in the bible is psalm 34:8. That verse in the Bible says, "O taste and see that the Lord is good: blessed is the man that trusteth in him." Revelation 22:17 says, "Come let him take of the water of life freely." When a man or women partakes of the water of life and the bread of heaven there soul will be instantly satisfied. Jesus is everything you and I need, and when we accept him he will give us all the guidance and vision that one could ever desire. Jesus is sweet to the taste, easy on the eyes, and satisfying to the soul. When people begin to walk with Jesus they will find everything they need wrapped into one. He is altogether wonderful in every single way. Jesus came that we might have life, and have it more abundantly. The Lord is constantly blessing his own in new and exciting forms and fashions. This story I will now give is a prime example of his goodness towards his children. It may seem small but it touched this old sinner's heart. Allow me to show you how good the Lord is.

One night while I was playing with my baby girl, my wife told me she had to run and get some groceries. Before she left that night she asked me twice if I needed anything. At that point in time nothing came to my mind so I said no thanks. Around fifteen minutes after she left I started to crave a hot chocolate from Tim Horton's. As I went to pick up the phone to call her the Holy Spirit told me not to call but rather pray for it. Immediately I dropped my head and prayed that God would lay it on her to stop and get me one. After I prayed a sudden peace came over me and I knew it would come true. Around an hour later my wife walked in our house carrying two Tim Horton hot chocolates and some donuts. My first response was thank you Erin, and secondly I said God is good.

Let me just say that many will look at that story and say that is just by luck that things turned out like that. My response to that would be if it were only once or twice I could see it, but if it is on a daily basis then it must be God doing it. O taste and see that the Lord is good while you still have breath in your body. He will satisfy your every desire in a glorious new way.

## *Scriptures Chapter 8*

Psalm 34:8 "O taste and see that the Lord is good: Blessed is the man that trusteth in him."

Revelation 22:17 "And the Spirit and the bride say, come. And let him that heareth say, come. And let him that is athirst come. And whosoever will, let him take the water of life freely."

John 10:10 "The thief cometh not, but to steal, and to kill, and to destroy: I am come that they might have life, and that they might have it more abundantly."

# CHAPTER 9
# DIVINE PROTECTION SENT FROM ABOVE

The Book of all books is filled with examples of God sending divine protection for His children. One might remember Daniel in the lion's den or Joseph in the pit. Maybe you could recall David when he was running from Saul or when he fought Goliath. In Psalms 18:2 it says, "The Lord is my Rock, and my fortress, and my deliver; my God, my strength, in whom I trust; my buckler, and the horn of my salvation, and my high tower." Isaiah 43:2 also tells us that, "When we pass through the waters, I will be with thee, and when we walk through the fire we shall not be burned." In Psalms 23:4 it says, "Yea though I walk through the valley of the shadow of death I will fear no evil, for thou art with me." A little further along in Psalms 27:1 it reads, "The Lord is my light and my salvation; whom shall I fear? The Lord is the strength of my life; of whom shall I be afraid?" We also see in II Timothy 1:7 it states, "That God hath not given us the spirit of fear; but of Power, and of love, and of a sound mind."

We have the victory, and God enjoys making that known in the life of His children. When Satan wanted to attack Job, he accused God of setting up a hedge around him. Jesus Christ will defend us, protect us, and watch over us if we belong to him. He is a wonderful father and He has a way of keeping trouble at bay, more often than not.

In the line of work that I do, I am surrounded by danger on a daily basis. As I work on the road, I often find myself dodging traffic and avoiding accidents. I have had many close calls over the years and only, by the grace of God, am I still alive. Let me give you a little story that will be a blessing to you.

One Wednesday night, as the prayer requests were being taken, I remember asking the church for divine protection for the rest of the work week. Every time I look over the pages of my life, I realize that prayer has always been my saving grace.

This particular night I had to drive a separate car home then my family. On the way home I wanted to take the scenic route and enjoy the beauty of nature. I recall listening to gospel music and it was getting hard to see. All of the sudden I happened to look to my right and a deer was standing on the side of the road. The deer looked me in my eye and stood still like a statue. It was almost like God commanded that deer to stand still until I drove by.

Shortly after I drove by I saw the deer seemly unfreeze and gently walk across the road behind me. My mind went back to that prayer request taken at church forty minutes earlier and how I had asked for protection. James said that, "The effectual fervent prayer of a righteous man availeth much." I challenge you to turn back a few pages of your life and recall how many times God has sheltered you through life. Most Christians I know have stared death in the face often, but something always keeps them safe. Let me just say John had it right when he said "No man is able to pluck them out of my Fathers hand."

## Scriptures Chapter 9

Psalm 18:2 "The Lord is my Rock, and my fortress, and my deliverer; my God, my strength, in whom I will trust; my buckler, and the horn of my salvation, and my high tower."

Psalm 23:4 "Yea, though I walk through the valley of the shadow of death, I will fear no evil: for thou art with me: thy rod and thy staff they comfort me."

Psalm 23:6 "Surely goodness and mercy shall follow me all the days of my life: and I will dwell in the house of the Lord forever."

Isaiah 43:2 "When thou passeth through the waters, I will be with thee: and through the rivers, they shall not overflow thee: when thou walkest through the fire, thou shalt not be burned; neither shall the flame kindle upon thee."

Psalm 27:1 "The Lord is my light and my salvation; whom shall I fear? The Lord is the strength of my life; of whom shall I be afraid?"

2 Timothy 1:7 "For God hath not given us the spirit of fear; but of power, and of love, and of a sound mind."

Job 1:10 "Hast not thou made a hedge about him, and about his house, and about all that he hath on every side? Thou hast blessed the work of his hands, and his substance is increased in the land."

James 5:16 "Confess your faults one to another, and pray one for another, that ye may be healed. The effectual fervent prayer of a righteous man availeth much."

John 10:28 "And I give unto them eternal life; and they shall never perish, neither shall any man pluck them out of my Father's hand."

# CHAPTER 10
# THE ALMIGHTY JUDGMENT OF GOD

People all over this country have a warped concept of who God really is. Many hold to the theory that God needs us and that He would be hurting without our presence on planet earth. May I say to those who believe like this, you have been misguided by someone's false teaching somewhere along life's road. Calvary proves, beyond a shadow of a doubt, the love of God, but always remember that God is a God of anger as well. Psalm 90:7 says, "For we are consumed by thine anger, and by thy wrath are we troubled." Preachers are always quick to point out the love of God and they should, but there are just as many verses on His anger and fury throughout the Bible to balance it out. The average person I speak with cringes when I mention the judgment of God, but that does not change the reality of the truth.

It is sad to say that good men will argue with me, until they are blue in the face, about the thought of God's patience running out in a person's life. Mankind wants to jump over verses of this caliber because they are so worried about offending people. I have learned that no matter how gracious or sweet your words are someone, somewhere, will always find fault anyways. We cannot please everyone so just tell the truth whether they agree with you or not. God is angry with the wicked every day. Sometimes His patience runs out and His hammer drops after all other avenues of mercy are exhausted. Please allow me to express what I mean with the rest of this chapter.

Not long ago, at my parent's house, a conversation took place

33

that made the hair on my neck stand up. A man that I am close with asked me if God really kills people once they cross spiritual lines. When he asked this question I responded by giving him a number of verses and examples that were earthshaking. After around a solid hour of examples about God slaying folks you could absolutely feel the presence of God in a remarkable way. The man I was talking with was shaking and looked very sick. Once I noticed how it was affecting him, I quickly ended the conversation out of respect for the man.

Shortly after this conversation was complete I spoke with my father and he said, "Tony I want to show you something." My dad took me to a nearby table, sat me down, and handed me a Bible from the year 1856. He told me to flip through its pages and tell me what you think. As I took that old Bible I opened it up and it opened straight to I Samuel 2:6 and this is how it read, "The Lord KILLETH and he maketh alive: he bringeth down to the grave, and bringeth up." My eyes fell upon that verse and the power of God fell on me.

In my private studies that week the Lord allowed me to read that verse around twenty times prior to opening my Dad's old Bible. I Samuel 2:33-34 teaches that God was so angry at Eli and his two sons that he promised to kill them in the flower of their age. Be very careful not to grieve God's Spirit too often throughout the days of your life because it can do you much harm. Always remember this verse as you conduct your life, Psalm 7:13b"He hath also prepared for him the instruments of death; He ordaineth his arrows against the persecutors." God is indeed a God of Love but He is also very much a God of judgment.

## Scriptures Chapter 10

Psalm 7:11 "God judgeth the righteous, and God is angry with the wicked every day."

Ephesians 4:30 "And grieve not the holy Spirit of God, whereby ye are sealed unto the day of redemption."

Psalm 90:7 "For we are consumed by thine anger, and by thy wrath are we troubled."

1 Samuel 2:6 "The Lord killeth, and maketh alive: he bringeth down to the grave, and he bringeth up."

Psalm 7:13 "He hath also prepared for him the instruments of death; he ordaineth his arrows against the persecutors."

# CHAPTER 11
# THE OVERSHADOWING OF THE HOLY GHOST

There is nothing more powerful in this world then the overshadowing of the Holy Ghost. When God's spirit is present and moving, fear strikes the heart of man. In the Old Testament when the ark would go before the people, they would shake and quake with fear. In the New Testament, when Paul was preaching to Felix, the word of God says he trembled. Daniel 5 records that when the Holy Ghost showed up that Belshazzar's knees smote together. When the great Jonathon Edwards would preach during the great awakening, history says that people would have a fear of dropping off into hell before the morning light. The bible teaches in Luke that Mary was overshadowed by the Holy Ghost as she was carrying the Son of God. Hebrews 10:31 says "It is a fearful thing to fall into the hands of a living God."

When God's spirit is present in a service; it becomes hard to breathe, sinners grip the pews, palms get sweaty, and hearts skip a beat. When God's Holy Ghost overshadows a service you will never forget it till the day you die. God's spirit comes when it wants to and it leaves when it wants to. God's Spirit does not ask permission and it is always felt by those around him. It is breathtaking and scary when His presence can be felt. Many lose sleep, pace around, and hide in fear when the Spirit of God is doing His' work. The story you are about to read is powerful, and it will cause you to search your inner being. Till this day it remains one of the most amazing heart pounding stories that I could ever tell. God seemed to visit us that day and I do not know if I have ever felt a presence so strong.

A few years back, God opened up a door to witness to a young man named Shane, and it was beyond enlightening. From the time I got in the truck till the time I left the truck great power filled the air. Shane had been at the company for weeks, yet I had never had a chance to speak to him before. Shane was very nice and very interested in God. He would ask a question and I would answer with a number of verses and real stories. With each passing moment the feeling of conviction got stronger and stronger as I presented the gospel to him. Around twenty five minutes into our ride; it was so powerful we could hardly even shallow. It felt like God himself was sitting between us that night. Shane was shaking and I was as well. He looked at me with a look of fear and asked, "So you really think God is real?" My reply to him was sure I do and that is why as I pointed at the street sign in front of us.

Out of all the names that the street could have been it happened to be Jerusalem Street. We had been driving in the sticks when this took place and I was just about to tell him a story from Jerusalem to prove God was real. The timing was impeccable and the feeling was unmatched. As I concluded telling him this story we continued to drive and as we looked up, the next street was called Church Street. At this point God's anointed power was everywhere and silence filled the whole area. As we turned the corner we happened to arrive at our destination in Saline Michigan. When we stepped out of the truck to see if someone would show us where to place our signs something incredible happened. A drunken man staggered up to me and said one curse word and stopped immediately. He looked me straight in my eyes and said, "I can't do this you're a good man." God's power hit that man like a ton of bricks and he staggered away in shame. God's divine presence filled that entire area in a Holy way. Personally I have never seen anything like it before.

After this stunning incident took place we received word of where to place the signs. The person in charge led us around the back of a bar and asked us if we could lay the signs in a certain spot. To our surprise in the spot where we were told to lay our signs a church was painted on the back of the bar. In my thirty two years of living I have never seen a church painted on the back of a bar, but we did that night. Five seconds later I saw Shane bow his head and I asked him if he was alright. Shane then looked at me and said, "Just listen." He then turned up the radio and out of all the songs that could have come on it was a song called "Jesus Take the Wheel." We both shook our heads and unloaded our signs. Time almost seemed to stand still and we were speechless.

After our work was complete we had one final place to go and God's Spirit grew stronger and stronger. On the way to Chelsea there was a parade going on and the Gideon's were right in the middle of that crowd passing out bibles. When Shane had seen this, for some reason he made a sharp right turn and there was a huge cross staring us in the face. The power of God seemed like a shadow all around us and we will never forget that feeling. Shane actually called his mother that night and wanted to get things right with her. He told me that he needed to tell her that he loved her because he wasn't sure if he would make out of the truck alive. He didn't accept Christ but the Power was so real.

After we went home that night I was still shaking over what happened in that truck. It almost felt like walking through a page of the Bible that night. May we all have moments when God pays us a special visit from above. The Bible says in Psalm 8:4, "What is man, that thou art mindful of him? And the son of man that thou visitest him." There is nothing that can compare to a visit from the Holy One. Shane and I will never forget it throughout all of eternity.

This chapter would not be complete without this little side note. Around a month after this incident took place I was at a local barbershop and a precious Mexican lady was cutting my hair. This lady was very sweet and very friendly to all. As I went to tell her the above mentioned story she stopped me and said, "Tony do you know where I was born?" To be honest I had no earthy idea. Her answer totally shocked me when she said ,"Tony I was born in downtime Jerusalem." Out of all the places in the world that may have been the last place I would have guessed. Immediately my mind went back to that night with Shane. What a powerful moment in time. God is real my friends.

## Scriptures Chapter 11

Daniel 5:6 "Then the King's countenance was changed, and his thoughts troubled him, so that the joints of his loins were loosed, and his knees smote one against another."

Hebrews 10:31 "It is a fearful thing to fall into the hands of a living God."

Psalm 8:4 "What is man, that thou art mindful of him? And the son of man, that thou visitest him?"

# CHAPTER 12
# BEHOLD THE MESSIAH

When John the Baptist came on the scene, with divine power on his life, he tried his absolute best to point the crowds to the Messiah. All of John's statements seemed to come from heaven, and every word he spoke got people's attention. The power of God flowed through his body and multitudes were coming from everywhere. One day according to the book of John 1:29 as people were in total awe of his message; he stopped and pointed toward the Messiah. As the people turned to see who he was pointing at, John said these words, "Behold the lamb of God that taketh away the sin of the world."

All the attention John had been receiving went directly to Jesus in a split second of time. John was showing the world that his sole purpose for living was to point others to the Messiah. When the Lord is lifted up great things will begin to happen. Lives will be touched, hearts will be mended, and souls will be redeemed. There are not many different roads to heaven but there is only one road to heaven and that is through Jesus Christ.

We as Christians need to get out of the way and allow Jesus to be magnified to a lost and dying world. Christ doesn't need us, but we sure do need him. He is the reason for the season, and we should lift him up every chance we get. John 12:32 says, "If I be lifted up from the earth, will draw all men unto me." The great old song says it best when it says, "Look and live my brother live, look to Jesus now and live."

I have always been taught that Israel is the center of the earth, and Calvary is the center of the universe. Jesus Christ is the pinnacle of everything that really matters, and his blood will never lose its power. May this powerful story point you to the Messiah in a glorious way, and touch your heart for His glory.

Every Christmas season, the most powerful musical in the world, takes center stage around this country. The musical is Handel's Messiah and it has impacted thousands for Christ. Every year it is performed, and every time it moves the soul. Fredrick Handel wrote the entire piece in just a few days, and it stirs the soul like nothing else can. Through the power of music, God's word is quoted in a magical way.

The first time I heard it I could do nothing but weep over its beauty. During the last song of this musical, the whole building rises to their feet, to give God the glory. Nothing on earth can compare to the feeling you have on the inside when the Hallelujah Chorus is being sung. Personally I believe every Christian living, owes it to their self, to see Handel's Messiah at least once in their lifetime. Powerful is the only word I could use to describe it. Allow me to tell you what happened not long ago in my life.

As I was working, in Detroit picking up cones, we stopped by an old church and seen a sign advertizing that Handel's Messiah was coming in December. While I was looking at the sign, a young man came to my mind that had never seen Handel's Messiah before. I then bowed my head and asked that God would use someone to buy that man tickets to Handel's Messiah. My prayer was simply this, "Lord please give someone a burning desire to buy those tickets for that young man."

Around a week later, after church, I received a text message from that same young man that I prayed for. He revealed to me that my father came to him that night and said from out of nowhere the Lord told him to buy them both Handel's Messiah tickets. This man also said my dad promised to take him out to eat after the concert was over. My heart was overwhelmed by the convicting power of God, and I humbly give him the honor He deserves.

Sinner friend, it only takes one look at the Messiah and your life can take a drastic turn for the better. My heart will be forever thankful for Isaiah 9:6. The bible says in this verse, "For unto us a child is born, unto us a Son is given: and the government shall be upon his shoulder: and his name shall be called Wonderful, Counselor, The mighty God, The everlasting Father, the Prince of Peace."

## *Scriptures Chapter 12*

John 1:29 "The next day John seeth Jesus coming unto him, and saith, Behold the Lamb of God, which taketh away the sin of the world."

John 12:32 "And I, if I be lifted up from the earth, will draw all men unto me."

Isaiah 9:6 "For unto us a child is born, unto us a son is given: and the government shall be upon his shoulder: and his name shall be called Wonderful, Counselor, The mighty God, the everlasting Father, The Prince of Peace."

# CHAPTER 13
# A MAN'S BEST FRIEND

There is a special bond found throughout the pages of time between animals and mankind. It was Adam's job to name the animals, which God had created, and our connection with animals is undeniable. In the book of Genesis the bible teaches that before God ever sent a universal flood Noah called all the animals into the ark. Proverbs 12:10 teaches that a righteous man regardeth the life of his beast. God created animals for many different reasons, but one of the greatest reasons was to be a companion with man. God used Balaam's ass to rebuke his own master. God sent the raven's to minister to Elijah in his time of need.

Often times God uses animals to convey a message. In the book of Jonah God used a whale to get his man's attention. In the gospels he used a cock crowing thrice to signify Peter's denial of the Savior. All throughout the bible animals play an important role. After all Christ is the lion of the tribe of Judah, Satan is as a roaring lion, and we will all ride on white horses one day if we are saved. Jesus is the great Shepherd and we are his sheep.

There is a definite connection between humans and animals that has stood the test of time. According to many animal lovers perhaps the greatest connection between Man and Beast is the connection of dogs and there owners. It is commonly referred to as man's best friend. When you have a good faithful dog, they almost become like a family member. We had a dog name Max growing up and we were blessed to have him for many years. As time went on he became very special to us and we loved him dearly. There is an unexplainable relationship between man and dog that we can't put our finger on. For the rest of this chapter I will give you a story that will strengthen your faith in Christ. This is a feel good story and I pray you will gain hope through reading it.

One day, shortly after I arrived home from work, our phone rang and it was my wife's mother. As my wife picked up the phone there was weeping on the other line because her dog Marley had come up missing. Marley is one of the sweetest dogs I've ever known and she is important to the entire family. We wondered how we could help so my wife made up fliers with Marley's picture on it. Hours and hours passed but there was still no sign of Marley anywhere. My wife's mother was worried as two hours turned into five hours without little Marley returning home. At around 10:00 p.m. that night my daughter Hope and I said a quick prayer for Marley to return back home. At 11:01 p.m., as I was lying in bed with my wife, a peace came over me and I told her Marley was home safe and sound. It was at 11:05 p.m. that our phone rang and I told my wife it was her mother telling us that Marley was with them again. Sure enough it was my mother -in- law telling us, with excitement, that her baby had returned home.

When I think about this story it reminds me that God has everything under control and we need not fear when he is near. A dog may be man's best friend physically, but God is man's best friend spiritually. What a friend we have in Jesus. The old song says He whispers sweet peace to me and He sure did that night.

## Scriptures Chapter 13

Proverbs 12:10 "A righteous man regardeth the life of his beast: but the tender mercies of the wicked are cruel."

1 Kings 17:4 "And it shall be, that thou shalt drink of the brook; and I have commanded the ravens to feed thee there."

Proverbs 18:24 "A man that hath friends must show himself friendly; and there is a friend that sticketh closer than a brother."

Matthew 12:40 "For as Jonah was three days and three nights in the whale's belly; so shall the Son of man be three days and three nights in the heart of the earth."

# CHAPTER 14
# WHERE IS
# THE LORD GOD OF ELIJAH?

When you start to list men throughout history, who had a touch of God on their life, you will not get very far until the name of Elijah is mentioned. Elijah's power with God was something to behold and it's something we should strive after. The bible tells us that Elijah brought down fire, brought a young boy back to life, and was caught up into heaven with a chariot of fire. As we examine his power, we must ask ourselves where is this power today?

James declared unto us, in the word of God, that Elijah was no different than us. Today we can still have this power if we hunger and thirst after it. In this chapter I will prove to you that God desires to give you the power of Elijah; if you will follow him with all your heart, soul, and mind. This chapter is also clear proof that God's power is present and with us today.

One day, as I was reading the bible at work, I found myself in 1 Kings, Chapter 18. This is the chapter where Elijah brought down the fire from heaven. As I was reading this great chapter my coworker and I heard a report on the news. The news reporter explained how our President and his workers of darkness were once again trying to steal religious liberties from Christians. When I heard this news I looked at my coworker and said, "I'm sick of this government trying to rob us of what God has given us." My coworker looked at me and said, "You better watch what you say Tony, they are probably listening." When he made that statement a power from above fell on me and I gave him a direct response he would never forget. I said, "Sir, I will gladly meet him on top of Mount Carmel right now and we can have a showdown on the mountain." Once those words left my lips a power from the glory world filled my soul and it lasted the rest of that day. Shortly after I made that statement amazing things started taking place.

First my boss notified me that I would be working a double shift, which I was not prepared for. My thoughts quickly went to 1 Kings 17, where God fed Elijah for three and a half years with a raven. I recall looking up into heaven and asking God to sustain me like Elijah. Immediately after making this request I looked down and staring back at me was a one dollar bill. I quickly picked it up and God spoke to me and said there is your drink. Directly after this happened I took a few more steps and I found another dollar and God said there is your snack. Shortly after finding that second dollar I happened to look around again and there was one last dollar and immediately my eyes fastened onto the words In God We Trust.

After all this took place I hurried back to the shop to tell my co-worker what had just happened. When I returned to the shop I saw a note with a ten dollar bill that said, "Tony get gas with this money." At this point the power of Elijah filled my soul as strong as it ever had before and his glory was all around me. Right after this took place I looked up at the clock and noticed that it was time for my second shift to begin.

I arrived at the school and a voice whispered inside my soul to go get a drink with the dollar God gave me. I quickly hurried to the break room and placed that dollar in the pop machine and God told me to get a Coke. At this particular time the Coke - Cola company had been placing share a coke with someone on their bottles and then it gave a name. As I pushed the button I received my coke and stood in amazement as I read the words Share a coke with Elijah. When I read that phrase it overwhelmed me. Out of all the names that could have been on the bottle that day, God made sure it was the name Elijah. I believe by God telling me to buy that coke and it being Elijah he was putting his stamp of approval on the statement I made earlier that day. The divine power I felt at that moment was priceless and I still have the bottle to this day as a reminder of what God did.

When my days are over and people form different views about my life, I want them to remember this story. It does not matter what people say about us it only matters what God knows about us. Thank God for his power and his Amazing Grace. Two weeks after that story had happened a dear woman took my book, Walking on the Water with Jesus, all around Israel and took many photos. She told me that when she went up on top of Mount Carmel with my book a power hit her like never before. She said, "Tony the power I felt that day is impossible to put into words." Many still ask the question, Where is the Lord God of Elijah? I hope after reading this chapter it cleared up that question for you.

## Scriptures Chapter 14

2 Kings 2:14 "And he took the mantle of Elijah that fell from him, and smote the waters, and said, Where is the Lord God of Elijah? And when he also had smitten the waters, they parted hither and thither: and Elisha went over."

Matthew 5:6 "Blessed are they which hunger and thirst after righteousness: for they shall be filled."

# Chapter 15
# What a
# Great God We Serve

For me to try to put into words just how great our God is seems impossible. His power is infinite, His grace is overwhelming, and His mercy is to all generations. The love of God is never failing, and His salvation is never ending. No words can describe this great God we serve. There is a song I learned as a child that says this "Wonderful grace of Jesus greater then all my sin, how shall my tongue describe it, where shall my praise begin." Thousands throughout the ages of time have tried to comprehend this God supreme, but we all fail to grasp the whole picture.

Psalm 48:1 says, "Great is the Lord, and greatly to be praised, in the city of our God, in the mountain of his holiness." Revelation 5:13 says ,"Every creature which is in heaven, and on the earth, and under the earth, and such are in the sea, and all that are in them, heard I saying, blessing, and honour, and glory, and power, be unto him that sitteth upon the throne, and unto the Lamb for ever and ever." Titus 2:13 says it like this, "Looking for that blessed hope, and glorious appearing of the great God and our Savior Jesus Christ." We, as His children, are longing for that wondrous day when we shall behold the Lord once and for all.

The Lord has given us hope, joy, peace, assurance, and everything we need as we wait for that glad day. The Lord has also given us divine light, His instruction manual, and His eternal promises as we labour here below. Our God is known as the Great Shepherd, the living bread, the Lamb of God, and the door to heaven. One of my favorite verses in the bible is Romans 8:32 which reveal's His greatness in a marvelous way. Romans 8:32 says, " He that spared not his own Son, but delivered him up for us all, how shall he not with him also freely give us all things?" Please permit me to give you a story that displays God's greatness in a very loving way. This story is an awesome picture of how God has pity on His children.

Something took place not long ago that is almost impossible to believe, but I have two witnesses that this indeed came to pass. Only our great God could make this possible and I praise his holy name for it. Let me declare exactly what God hath done for my soul.

Through the years, a host of different people have asked me if I had anything I would like one day as a gift. My answer has always been no, just a dipping dot ice cream machine. When I made this statement everyone would laugh, but I was always serious about what I said. Psalm 115:3 says, "But our God is in the heavens: he hath done whatsoever he hath pleased." The bible teaches us never to limit God, and I believe He can do the unthinkable for me.

One day I told my wife that I believed God was going to put it on someone's heart to give me a dipping dot machine, because he loved me. My wife did not give me much of a reaction, but if God be for us who can be against us. Around ten months later, my boss called me in his office with some amazing news. He said, "Tony, you won't believe this but they are giving away a free dipping dot machine and it is yours if you want it." My heart overflowed with joy as he told me the news. Although I've always wanted a dipping dot machine, I had to turn it down because I had limited space at home.

Isn't it amazing how God will bless us with things that are near and dear to our hearts? The bible asks this question "is anything to hard for God?" The answer to that question is no and I hope this story proves that to you. Over the years God has manifested His kindness towards me in many different ways. This story in particular proves His interest in me personally. What a great God we serve.

## *Scriptures Chapter 15*

Romans 8:31 "What shall we then say to these things? If God be for us, who can be against us?"

Psalm 115:3 "But our God is in the heavens: he hath done whatsoever he hath pleased."

Titus 2:13 "Looking for that blessed hope, and the glorious appearing of the great God and our Savior Jesus Christ:"

Romans 8:32 "He that spared not his own Son, but delivered him up for us all, how shall he not with him also freely give us all things?"

# CHAPTER 16
# A SUPER BLESSING

This story is almost beyond description but I will try my best to put it into words. Anyone who knows me personally knows that I'm a big sports fan. When I was a child I dreamed of being like Magic Johnson or Barry Sanders. I would play or watch sports for hours a day, but today I would much rather be like Peter or Paul. With that said one fact still remains, I still enjoy a good game as well.

Psalms 37:4 says "Delight thyself in the Lord; and he shall give thee the desires of thy heart." If you're a sports fan, a Christian or just someone who likes good stories, this one is for you. To this day it still thrills my soul and blesses me over and over again. It happened while I was at work one day; and God performed a miracle for me that I would have never dreamed could or would have happened. Let me tell you what took place.

It was around two in the afternoon, when I started a conversation with a man. He mentioned that at his other job they would give him the rare opportunity to work at the Super Bowl hanging up different banners. As we were talking the Lord told me to get ready for a major blessing that would be coming my way. At the time I had no idea what that blessing would be, but I prepared my mind for something great.

Around two hours later I was talking to another man about work, and in the middle of his sentence he switched gears and asked if I liked sports. I then replied that I did. He then said, "I don't know why but something just told me to give you an item that was given to me." I then said to him "what would that be?" and his answer shocked me. He said

I want to give you a Super Bowl football from the Super Bowl that was played in Detroit. I stood speechless because rarely do people give stuff like that away. He insisted and I couldn't change his mind.

To be honest I was prepared for a big blessing but not a Super Bowl football. God sure does love to bless His own. What makes this even more amazing is the fact that early that same morning something set the stage for all this to take place. At 9:04 a.m. I sent my wife a text that said have a SUPER day. Never, before that day, have I ever said that phrase but for some reason I said it that day. Little did I know that morning God was going to bless me with a SUPER day as well. The football was beautiful and this story still helps me to this very day. Psalms 21:2 says "Thou hast given him his heart's desire and hast not with-holden the requests of his lips." Selah.

## *Scriptures Chapter 16*

Psalm 37:4 "Delight thyself also in the Lord: and he shall give thee the desires of thine heart."

Psalm 21:2 "Thou hast given him his heart's desire, and hast not withholden the request of his lips. Selah."

# CHAPTER 17
# MY HELP
# COMETH FROM THE LORD

Every single day of my life people ask me this question how can you trust God the way that you do? My response to that question is clear I am not trusting in my own weak abilities, but rather in the abilities of an infinite powerful God that has never failed. When we realize that He has been everywhere and has seen everything, we will also understand that He watches over His own as well. God has promised to hide us under the shadow of the almighty. He is our sword and shield and we are kept by the power of God. If we serve the Lord and trust in His abilities He will move heaven and earth on our behalf. Remember He is the Alpha and Omega and with Him all things are possible. He is a faithful and just God, and He is touched with the feelings of our infirmities. He guides, protects, provides, and overshadows those who walk with Him. When we look at life with that view we will have no problem trusting Him for our every need. Our God is in the heavens, and there is nothing to hard for Him. With the remainder of this chapter I will give you a story that will show the goodness of God once again.

As I was working, a short while back, I experienced a very trying day. Besides being very sick, I also had a bad headache and backache at the same time. About midway through the day, I recall having a desire to call my mom to ask her to pray for me. Calling off work was out of the question because we were hurting for money at the time. My sweet mother was kind enough to offer to pay for a day off in which I declined.

My mother asked if I was sure and I told her that I have a God in heaven that will take care of me at church tonight. When those words left my lips I was absolutely sure that God would take care of me that night. Peace flooded my soul and I just knew a miracle would take place. Sure enough that night at church God performed a miracle in a wonderful way. That evening I set my bible down on the pew and headed for the back to use the restroom. When I made it back to my pew I found that there was a twenty dollar bill sitting on my Bible that wasn't there before. When my eyes laid hold upon this miracle my mind thought about my great God who sitteth upon his throne.

When we limit God we are only hurting ourselves. May I submit unto you that God has never failed one time, and it is impossible for Him to lie? God is always able to help us but only if we get out the way and allow him too. We have a God that knows the beginning from the end and he will always supply our every need.

## *Scriptures Chapter 17*

Psalm 121:2 "My help cometh from the Lord, which made heaven and earth."

Luke 1:37 "For with God nothing shall be impossible."

Psalm 91:4 "He shall cover thee with his feathers, and under his wings shalt thou trust: his truth shall be thy shield and buckler."

Revelation 1:8 "I am Alpha and Omega, the beginning and the ending, saith the Lord, which is, and which was, and which is to come, the Almighty."

Psalm 37:25 "I have been young, and now am old; yet have I not seen the righteous forsaken, nor his seed begging bread."

# CHAPTER 18
# GOD IS ALWAYS PLEASED
# WITH COMPASSION

Nothing in this world pleases the heart of the Lord anymore then when people exercise compassion towards one another. Jude said that you will make an eternal difference in the kingdom of God if you will add this to your everyday life. Love is a power all its own and with it all the world can be at your disposal. Psalms 145:8 states that, "The Lord is full of compassion and great in mercy." Without love in our life, according to I Corinthians 13:2, we are nothing. God wants us to think on the cares of others throughout our existence on earth. When we live a life of compassion, God in return will allow people to return the favor someday. Every day of my life I look for ways to help others; because of that fact God uses others to help me. Although I could give you many stories to prove my point, I will give you one that should speak to your heart pretty clearly. Please allow God's spirit to open your heart to the need of helping others through this story.

My two favorite times of the year would have to be Thanksgiving and the Christmas seasons. During these few months, people actually display some good deeds and live like Christ would want them to live. Excitement fills the air and a good spirit can be felt. May we all remember that twenty two percent of the world lives in poverty and God has been very good to us.

Around this time of year I'm always trying to find new ways to help the less fortunate. It was five years ago that I had an idea to give my annual company turkey to a sweet lady who was struggling badly. Immediately after I received my turkey that year I drove to the trailer park, where she lived, and surprised her with a thirteen pound turkey for Thanksgiving. When I gave her the gift she began to cry, gave me a big hug and thanked me very deeply. As I left her porch I had a warm feeling inside and I felt like God was pleased with me.

Two years later, I was trying to raise funds for some needy kids and God remembered my kindness. Within one glorious hour three different people came up to me with turkeys for the children. My heart was blessed that day. Two of the men, who had given me their turkeys, told me they don't know why but something told them to give them to me. I believe that God in heaven smote their hearts and caused them to help me in a special way. Besides the turkeys that year, God allowed me to raise around one thousand six hundred dollars for poor needy kids. In turn the kids had a wonderful holiday season that year.

When you help the needy God will always send something your way. I am very glad, to this day, that I showed compassion on the needy because God rewarded me abundantly. The good Lord said in Acts 20:35, "It is better to give then to receive."

## Scriptures Chapter 18

Jude 22 "And of some have compassion, making a difference."

Psalm 145:8 "The Lord is gracious, and full of compassion; slow to anger, and of great mercy."

I Corinthians 13:2 "And though I have the gift of prophecy, and understand all mysteries, and all knowledge; and though I have all faith, so that I could remove mountains, and have not charity, I am nothing."

Acts 20:35 "It is more blessed to give than to receive."

# CHAPTER 19
# TIS SO SWEET
# TO TRUST IN JESUS

Without question, one of the greatest gospel songs to have ever been penned is the song Tis so Sweet to Trust in Jesus. Its peaceful words and Godly truths have a way of claiming a troubled soul. The lady that wrote this song was Miss Louisa Stead and she was a missionary for many years. Her life was filled with letdowns, setbacks, and heartbreaks. Although life at times was very rough, Miss Stead had a heart for God and she trusted Jesus for her every need.

Sometimes trusting the Lord through hardships in life is difficult but Miss Stead shows us the formula in this song. The fourth verse in her song reads like this, "I'm so glad I learned to trust thee, precious Jesus, Savior friend, and I know that thou art with me, wilt be with me till the end." Miss Stead was showing us that though we may not have all the answers, we serve a God who does. May we all live in faith trusting Christ every step of the way.

The bible teaches that He is a friend at all times, and He will never leave thee or forsake thee. Sometimes things come our way that totally take us off guard and bring us to our knees. During these times in our life, we must understand that the trail of our faith is more precious than gold. God has a reason for everything done in our life and we must trust him at all times. It will be a special day in our lives when we learn to walk by faith not by sight. The bible says, "Draw nigh to God, and he will draw nigh unto you." When we trust the Lord with all our heart, good things will happen. Let me give you a marvelous story that will glorify the God we serve.

One day at work, during the month of December, God answered a prayer very rapidly for me. The Christmas season was upon us, and it was very busy at my company. My boss asked me to empty the trash in the office and I said, "No problem sir." While I was in the process of emptying the trash, I came to the office break room where God was about to prove himself to me. On the break room table sat a large display of candy, cheese, and a huge white chocolate pretzel, which caught my attention. I remember feeling funny about asking for the pretzel so instead I bowed my head right there and then and asked God to move on someone's heart to give it to me. Immediately after the prayer I went to leave the office and one of my bosses came towards me very quickly. It was almost like God himself told him to move my way. This man looked at me and said, "Tony come with me." As I followed him that day, he took me right back to the place where that pretzel was and said to take the whole display including the white chocolate pretzel. In less than fifteen seconds, after I prayed, the Lord allowed me to take that basket home with me.

When you trust the Lord with a heart of faith the impossible becomes possible. When you really think about it the Lord has never failed one time. If we can't trust him who can we trust?

## *Scriptures Chapter 19*

Hebrews 13:5 "For he hath said, I will never leave thee, nor forsake thee."

Proverbs 3:5 "Trust in the Lord with all thine heart; and lean not unto thine own understanding."

Proverbs 17:17 "A friend loveth at all times, and a brother is born for adversity."

James 4:8 "Draw nigh unto God, and he will draw nigh unto you. Cleanse your hands, ye sinners; and purify your hearts, ye double minded"

# CHAPTER 20
# A VERY
# ENTERTAINING STORY

Christians are thought of by a lost world, to be boring and out of date. We are laughed at, scorned, rejected and despised. We are considered weak, brainwashed, and push over's. Whenever I hear these things I say to myself that is the furthest thing from the truth. Jesus is not weak, frail or the man upstairs. On the contrary He is powerful, alive and a miracle performer. God is known by the judgment which he executes. Jesus is very capable of handling any situation and He is just as amazing today as He was thousands of years ago.

To be honest, my life is not boring in any way. If you walked in my shoes for a day you would see this statement to be true. God allows me to walk in faith, power and victory through his guidance. Every day of my life, God seems to be working and some things I witness are anything but boring. People on average do not read there bible and therefore they have a false concept of a real Christian. Many tried to get rid of Moses but they didn't have a chance to run off God's man. Peter was ignorant and unlearned, but he was powerful and he walked on the water. Nabal tried to disrespect David, and ten days later his heart died within him.

A Christian that walks in the power of God is an unstoppable force. God will protect, shield, and defend his children at all costs. Joshua was an untouchable man and he won many battles with God. If I took the time I could give you hundreds of very entertaining stories I have heard that would thrill your heart to no end. Time after time God's hand has moved through the years and astounded those around me. With the rest of this chapter I will give you an entertaining story in every sense of the word.

A short time ago, something arose in my life that God knew all about. This circumstance required prayer and it was a need that was precious to me. One morning I called my mother and we prayed about this matter in private. Later on that day, as I was studying and recalling all God's blessings on my life, my phone rang. As I picked up the phone the voice I heard was from a man I hadn't heard from in months. He proceeded to tell me that they were moving to Florida and he had something he wanted to give me. After a few minutes of talking he revealed to me that he wanted to give me a free oak entertainment center with; a thirty six inch TV, a five disc DVD player, surround sound and other neat items. This gift was absolutely amazing. God saw fit to answer my prayer and it was a blessing from heaven.

Walking with God is the greatest honor that a man or women can receive, and there is nothing boring about it. When you are close to the Lord, blessings like this happen every day. The Bible teaches that if you walk with God his soul will delight in you. God will constantly bless those who do right in there life and bring honor to His holy name.

## Scriptures Chapter 20

Psalm 9:16 "The Lord is known by the judgment which he executeth:"

1 Samuel 25:38 "And it came to pass about ten days after, that the Lord smote Nabel, and he died."

Acts 4:13 "Now when they saw the boldness of Peter and John, and perceived that they were ignorant men, they marveled; and they took knowledge of them, that they had been."

# CHAPTER 21
# GOD CREATING SOMETHING OUT OF NOTHING

The Lord Jesus Christ has an amazing ability to create something out of nothing. In the book of Genesis he breathed into mans nostrils and Adam became a living soul. The Bible records that God said let there be light and there was light. In sixth days everything we see before us was created by a Holy God.

According to the Bible, everything is in a perfect balance and heaven is His throne and the earth is His footstool. God has the sun, moon, stars, galaxies, and planet earth in perfect harmony. The Bible declares that the earth hangs on nothing, and that he sitteh upon the circle of the earth. The heavens declare His handiwork, and the clouds are nothing more than the dust of his feet.

No human can properly explain the order of the universe or what makes man's heart tick. We must conclude that without God we can do nothing, and his ways are not are ways. Some things can never be explained with are feeble explanations, so we must realize that God is in the heavens and He has everything under control.

Often in the Bible, we find God turning nothing into something. God caused dead bones too live again, blinded eyes to see, and the dead to return to life. The Lord caused the deaf to hear, the red sea to part, and the broken to be made whole. God remains the only one with the ability to create hope in a hopeless situation.

One of my favorite stories, in the Bible, would have to be when the Lord told Peter to catch a fish, open up its belly, and take out money so that he and Peter could pay their taxes. God proved the wonder of His promise when the money was exactly what they needed to the penny. I have always stood amazed of that miracle ever since I was a child. The story that I will share now is very similar to that story.

One day, while driving with a man from my work, I could not help but notice that he was down in the dumps. I quickly tried to help him in any way I could, but nothing seemed to work. After I tried a few different things I bowed my head and asked the Lord to do something special for this man. Around ten minutes later, as we were picking up cones, the man lifted up a cone and found a fresh ten dollar bill. It was no doubt from the Lord and it was the cleanest ten dollar bill I had ever seen. The first thing I thought about was Peter and the fish story.

After work that day I called my mom with this amazing story. My mother was shocked and the first thing she said was, "Tony that reminds me of the story of Peter and the fish." I then replied mom that is what I thought too. The Lord answered my prayer that day and proved again that He can do whatever He wants to, whenever he wants to. Psalms 40:13 says this, "Be pleased, O Lord, to deliver me: O Lord, make haste to help me."

## *Scriptures Chapter 21*

Genesis 2:7 "And the Lord God formed man of the dust of the ground, and breathed into his nostrils the breath of life; and man became a living soul."

John 1:10 "He was in the world, and the world was made by him, and the world knew him not."

Isaiah 66:1 "Thus saith the Lord, The heaven is my throne, and the earth is my footstool: where is the house that ye build unto? And where is the place of my rest?"

Isaiah 40:17 "When the poor and needy seek water, and there is none, and there tongue faileth for thirst, I the Lord will hear them, I God of Israel will not forsake them."

Isaiah 40:22 "Let them bring them forth, and show us what shall happen: let them show the former things, what they shall be, that we may consider them, and know the latter end of them; or declare us things for to come."

Psalm 19:1 "The heavens declare the glory of God; and the firmament showeth his handiwork."

John 1:1 "In the beginning was the Word, and the Word was with God, and the Word was God."

John 15:5 "I am the vine, ye are the branches: He that abideth in me, and I in him, the same bringeth forth much fruit: for without me ye can do nothing."

Matthew 16:27 "For the Son of man shall come in the glory of his Father with his angels; and then he shall reward every man according to his works."

Nahum 1:3 "The Lord is slow to anger, and Great in power, and will not at all acquit the wicked: the Lord hath his why in the whirlwind and in the storm, and the clouds are the dust of his feet."

# CHAPTER 22
# AN OVERWHELMING RE-
# SPONSE FROM GOD

Whenever you determine to help one of God's anointed, you will find that the rewards will be endless. Often times, God will tip over His eternal blessing bucket and pour you out blessings that you will not be able to bear. Everything I am can be traced back to the many times I've helped God's men. Through my giving, God in return has opened up a treasure box of gifts that are hard to put into words.

The book of Romans says it like this "How beautiful are the feet of them that preach the gospel of peace." True men of God are rare, but they are precious in the sight of God. Whenever I am around a man of God, I try my best to support them in any way I can. Nothing on earth is more glorious than a man of God preaching with divine power from on high. God expects us to help his men any chance we get. They are indeed worthy of double honor, and you will only benefit the cause of Christ when you hold up the preacher's hands.

God's men get tired, weary, and stressed out; it is our job to assist them often. The great Dr. John Hamblin told me one day, and I quote, "Bro Tony, you are special in the eyes of God because you help His men. Just think, if we all had that testimony, what a difference we could make. God promises to reward us in a special fashion if we reach out by faith and encourage others. If this chapter does not prove to you that there are benefits to helping God's men, nothing will.

Last year the Lord gave me a great desire to help one of His very best servants in many different ways. Seemly all year I scrabbled, prayed and went crazy to find ways to encourage this awesome man of God. Money was very tight, but wherever there's a will there is a way. After much struggle and determination, God allowed me to help him in a powerful fashion. God gave me peace about my labors and he rewarded me in a way that is hard to understand.

Within two weeks of time, the Lord used fifteen different people to give me eighteen items. Please let me say that again, fifteen people gave me eighteen items. The following is a list of things that people either gave me or offered me:

My mother gave sixty dollars for gas, a man gave forty dollars to help my family, a lady gave fifty dollars and told me the Lord wanted her to do it, a lady from my church gave me two huge tub's of gummy bears and said enjoy, a man from my work made me a sign I was praying about for free, my father in law offered to buy us a dog for two hundred and fifty dollars but we had to turn it down, another man bought me two pops and refused to let me pay for them, a man of God gave me a priceless item and said I was a blessing, another lady bought me a frosty and told me God wanted her to, a sweet lady brought me in my own set of cookies that God told her to bake, a lady bought me a sweet tea that I gave to someone else, a man from my work gave me money and told me to get whatever I wanted, and finally a precious couple took my family to a nice place for dinner and paid for it.

Almost every one of those people assured me that God directed them to help me. Other little gifts were also given to me and my heart was very warmed in those two weeks.

Over the years the Lord has pampered me, and blessed me in many ways. My goal in writing this chapter is to point you to the one in whom all blessings flow. Jesus promises to reward those who help His servants. This chapter alone should silence all those who doubt the blessings that come from helping God's men. May we all be compelled to dig a little deeper and allow God to use us in this way. If we will do this, God promises to send a bundle of blessings our way, and the results will be staggering.

## *Scriptures Chapter 22*

Romans 10:15 "And how shall they preach, except they be sent? As it is written, how beautiful are the feet of them that preach the gospel of peace, and bring glad tidings of good things."

1 Timothy 5:17 "Let the elders that rule well be counted worthy of double honor, especially they who labor in the word and doctrine."

Malachi 3:10 "Bring ye all the tithes into the storehouse, that there may be meat in mine house, and prove me now herewith, saith the Lord of hosts, if I will not open up the windows of heaven, and pour you out a blessing, that there shall not be room enough to receive it."

# CHAPTER 23
# A VERY POWERFUL MOMENT

When the pages of my life unfold and my race on earth is complete; this story will stand as one of the best in my life. The presence of God could be strongly felt throughout the whole course of this day. I will never forget it till the day I die. When you read this story, I pray that it dawns on us just how much God really does love each and every one of us.

Psalms 40:17 records that even though we are poor and needy, the Lord thinketh upon us. This story contains a series of little blessings that cheered my heart in a beautiful way. The fact is every blessing whether great or small is amazing if it comes from God. This story proves that Christ loves us and he answers our prayers according to his will.

While my family and I were on vacation in Alpena Michigan, last summer, God showed up early one Sunday morning in a breath taking fashion. As we were checking out of the hotel that morning, to travel back to our home church, God had a series of blessings prepared that could only come from Him.

Over and over that weekend we had passed a candy machine and I never seemed to have change. My precious little girl looked at me with innocent eyes and asked if we could get some candy. I responded to her by saying, "Hope, Daddy doesn't have money but God does. Let's pray for a quarter." Hope said ok Dad and right there and then we prayed for just one quarter.

After we prayed we headed back to our room to gather our things. On the way there Hope saw the pop machines and had to hit the buttons. She then looked inside the machine and there was a new quarter sitting there just for us. When I saw that quarter I knew God had answered our prayer. We went directly back to that candy machine and got Hope her candy, and we were both on cloud nine.

When we made it back to the room I immediately called my mom and told her this amazing story. After talking to my mom for a few minutes I hang up the phone and, immediately after doing so, Hope came up to me with another quarter in her hand. Someone had given her another quarter. After witnessing this again I was praising the Lord for His goodness towards my family. The next thing I recall doing is calling my mom again with some more good news.

I hung up the phone for the second time and Hope came straight up to me and asked for another quarter. I told her not to get greedy and that God had already given her two quarters. I reminded her that prayer is the answer for everything and that we could pray for one last quarter. We then said a quick prayer and around ten seconds later we got a knock on the door. It was my sister in-law, and she was standing there with one more quarter for Hope. It seemed like God was present in the room with us that day. After all this took place I fell to my knees and thanked the Lord for what he had done.

Once we had loaded up the car, it was time for our long ride home. On the way home we saw a sight to behold that sticks out in my mind. What we saw was a seventy five foot statue of Christ holding the World in his hands. It was a reminder to me that God has this whole world in the palms of His hands. I'm thankful for the thought that we serve a God that knows the path we take and wipes away every tear we cry. When I had seen that statue I thought of the verse that says "Be still and know that I am God."

## Scriptures Chapter 23

Psalm 40:17 "But I am poor and needy; yet the Lord thinketh upon me: thou art my help and my deliverer; make no tarrying, O my God."

Psalm 46:10 "Be still, and know that I am God: I will be exalted among the heathen, I will be exalted in the earth."

# CHAPTER 24
# GOD VISITING A LADY FROM OUT OF NOWHERE

In the book of John, chapter four, we find a story that reveals how God deals with mankind. We read in the chapter about a woman, who lived a life of pleasure and sin, all the days of her life. She had already been married five times and the man she was involved with was not her husband. This woman was so vile that the other women in the city did not want anything to do with her, because of her ungodly life style. As far as we can tell she was perfectly content with her sin and she was determined to die in that condition. However, thank God we that know this story know that Jesus could see a different future in this ladies life. He showed up when she was least expecting him too. It just took one visitation from God to completely change this women's destination and gave her something worth living for.

When we study God's word, we quickly realize that the Holy Spirit appears to us when we are not even thinking about Him. There have been wicked drunkards, through the years, that have received a visit from God while walking down the street. There have been drug addicts that have fallen under heavy conviction through a praying mother, often over the centuries of time. Church kids have been known to have screamed out for mercy through a preacher who was thundering the word of God from his sacred desk. The Bible teaches that God does whatever He desire's, at any given time, to grab mankind's attention throughout life. There are hundreds of stories I could reveal that prove this is true, but I will give you one that happened recently that blessed my soul.

One day, at my work, the Lord directed me to call my mother and tell her what was on my heart. I felt like, in my heart, God was going to place it on someone's mind to buy me some Reese candies; so I could give them to a precious man of God. To most people this may seem strange but I wanted to be a blessing to a preacher and I believed it by faith. This conversation happened in private and only my mother and I knew about it.

Shortly after our conversation, on a Monday morning, a lady approached me and said I have a gift for you. She then gave me a bag and said, "I hope you enjoy Tony." To my amazement inside the bag there were Reese trees for me to enjoy. After she gave them to me she said there was a story she wanted to share with me. She told me as she was shopping the other day from out of nowhere my name came to her mind and she had a strong desire to buy me some Reese trees. She said she didn't know why but she couldn't leave that store until she bought those for me. Once she told me this story, I asked her what day and what time this took place. She told me at 3:45 p.m. on Thursday this took place. What was amazing about this was that on Thursday at 3:35 p.m. I told my mother this would happen.

God has a way of showing up at just the right time and in just the right fashion. The Bible tells us that when Saul was persecuting the church; that is when a holy God decided to appear in a way that totally shocked him. We as humans do not know how and we don't know why, but He will tell us all about it in the bye and bye. God is past finding out and I have learned, over the years, that He comes when he wants to, and He leaves when He wants to.

We must determine to respond to God when He shows up and speaks to our hearts. The pages of time are full of stories like this one you just examined and in God's own unique way, He will show up whenever He wishes to. The Bible says, "That I am God and there is none else." This is how God has always dealt with mankind. Ask yourself why God would deal with that lady about something like that. To be honest, I can't explain how God moves and deals with us, I just know He does. God's Spirit can move people in a way that nothing else can. The moving of God is a powerful force that is unexplainable with the human tongue, but it can be felt in the soul of man. That is the wonder and beauty of a thrice holy God.

## *Scriptures Chapter 24*

Isaiah 45:22 "Look unto me, and be ye saved, all the ends of the earth: for I am God, and there is none else."

John 4:29 "Come, see a man, which told me all things that I ever did: is not this the Christ?"

# CHAPTER 25
# THE JOY OF
# WALKING WITH THE LORD

The word of God teaches us in 3rd John verse 4 that a parent's greatest joy, this side of eternity, is that there children walk in truth. We, as children of God, are commanded to walk the straight and narrow path if we want the fullness of His power. God will give us all the tools possible to achieve this goal, but it is up to us to use them for His honor and glory. The biggest struggle that we face on a daily basis is the person that stares back at us in the mirror every morning. Often times we wander away from the Lord by our own free will. The Bible says in Psalm 4:3 that, "The Lord hath set apart the Godly for himself."

There have been rare men and women who have experienced great blessings of God through the years, and they would not change it for all the earth's riches. Enoch walked with God and he could feel the realness of the almighty in his life. Noah walked with God and he found grace in the eyes of the Lord. Charles Haddon Spurgeon walked with God and he became the most famous preacher in the World at the tender age of twenty. God has special things prepared for those who have paid the price and we can have them as well if we love God with all our hearts. If walking with the Lord was easy everyone would be doing it.

Last year alone, I'm thrilled to report, God allowed one hundred and eighty different people to give me three hundred and fifty six gifts in a single year. One family took us out to eat over fifty times. Please permit me to give you a typical day in the life of one who walks with God. This story is an example of how God blesses His own.

One day as my wife was walking into the bank and stranger asked her how old my daughter was. My wife responded by telling her that she was three years old. The women then told her to please wait there for a minute. The lady then went to her car to get something for my daughter. After a minute or so the stranger returned with a wrapped present in her hand and gave it to my daughter and drove away. When my little girl opened the present she found it was a Minnie Mouse puzzle. This gift was given to her by a perfect stranger. Later in the day, as my wife was driving in slippery conditions, she went to make a turn and she felt like God was keeping her car from turning. In a moment of time a car was going the wrong way on a one way street directly at her. God's hand of protection keep her from being in a head on collision and we give him the glory.

The day I just described to you is an example of an average day in a spirit filled Christian's life. Time would not allow me to explain to you the amazing wonders I behold on a daily basis and each day is a miracle in the making. Allow God to control your walk and talk of life and you too can know the joy of walking with the Savior. The old preacher had it right when he said, "God is good all the time."

Many of Gods children live far beneath their potential and they refuse to walk in Power. Sad to say they live a life of defeat instead of a life of victory. James 4:17 still says, "He that knoweth to do good and doeth it not to him it is sin." God has a great life planed for us if we will follow his leadership and yield to his Spirit.

## *Scriptures Chapter 25*

3 John 4 "I have no greater joy than to hear that my children walk in truth."

Psalm 4:3 "But know that the Lord hath set apart him that is Godly for himself: The Lord will hear when I call unto him."

Hebrews 11:5 "By Faith Enoch was translated that he should not see death; and was not found, because God had translated Him: for before his translation he had this testimony, that he pleased God."

Genesis 6:8 "But Noah found grace in the eyes of the Lord."

Ephesians 5:18 "And be not drunk with wine wherein is excess; but be ye filled with the Spirit;"

James 4:17 "Therefore to him that knoweth to do good, and doeth it not, to him it is sin."

# CHAPTER 26
# GOD TREATED ME LIKE A KING TWICE IN ONE WEEK

One of the greatest mysteries known to man is why the King of kings treats His own with such respect and honor. We find in the Bible that Jesus, the King, humbled himself and washed his disciple's feet. The Bible also teaches that this King led the children of Israel around for forty years, and made sure that every need they ever had was taken care of. Throughout the word of God, this King calls us his friends. We also find throughout the scriptures that Christ loves us deeply and cares for us always. Psalm 68:19 teaches that daily this King of Glory loads us up with benefits. Earlier in Psalm 18:19 it teaches that He has brought us into a large place, and that He delights in us.

Romans 8:17 tells us that we are joint heirs with Jesus Christ. God's word also declares that all things are created for our good pleasure. In Ephesians 1:3 it states, "That He has blessed us with all spiritual blessings in heavenly places in Christ." While in I Peter 1:4 it tells us, "We have an inheritance incorruptible and undefiled that fadeth not away, reserved in heaven for you."

The song writer had it right when he wrote, "Who am I that a King would bleed and die for?" Another great song puts it like this, "I'm a child of the King, and he loves me I know." Revelation 1:6 declares that He hath made us Priests and Kings through His blood. Although we can never understand such love, we must admit Christ treats us like royalty, if we are His children. The following are two short stories proving His love once again. May God use these stories to convince your heart, of His love, in a special way.

One morning, before we started work, my driver stopped at Burger King to grab some breakfast. As we went to order our food, my heart was set on a sausage and egg sandwich and a small drink. When I made it up to the register I discovered that we just missed breakfast, so instead I ordered a cheeseburger and a drink. To be honest with you, I was disappointed because, I was really looking forward to having that sausage and egg sandwich.

While I was waiting for my meal, I noticed the door opened, in the back behind the counter, and a lady was coming directly towards me with a sandwich in her hand. She looked right at me and said, "Sir would you like a sausage and egg sandwich? I would like to give it to you for free." My reply was, "Sure I would and thank you very much." It was four days later when my driver and I went back to that Burger King and witnessed another blessing from God.

Earlier that morning my wife and I agreed to be a little more careful on how we spent our money. We always seem to be scrapping by but we never go without. I remembered, just before I walked into Burger King that morning, I decided not to get a meal that day but only a soda. As I walked up to the register a lady was standing there like a solider of God. The lady looked at me and said, "What would you like today?" and I said I only wanted a large coke. The lady handed me a large cup and said that it was on the house today. It was almost like God himself told her to be ready to assist, because one of His servant's was coming through.

God's hand of mercy is very present in all our lives and it is up to us to notice when He is moving on our behalf. The precious old hymn says it like this "Why would he love me a sinner undone, why tell me why does he care." Let me close out this chapter with this verse. Psalm 24:7, "Lift up your heads, o ye gates; and be ye lift up, ye everlasting doors; and the King of Glory shall come in." When you open up your heart in submission to this King, He in return, will bring you into His royal family. To me that is a pretty good deal.

## *Scriptures Chapter 26*

1 Timothy 1:17 "Now unto the King eternal, immortal, invisible, the only wise God, be honor and glory forever and ever. Amen."

Psalm 68:19 "Blessed be the Lord, who daily loadeth us with benefits, even the God of our salvation. Selah."

Psalm 18:19 "He brought me forth also into a large place; he delivered me, because he delighted in me".

Romans 8:17 "And if children, then heirs; heirs of God, and joint-heirs with Christ; if so be that we suffer with him, that we may be also glorified together."

Ephesians 1:3 "Blessed be the God and Father of our Lord Jesus Christ, who hath blessed us with all spiritual blessings in heavenly places in Christ:"

1 Peter 1:4 "To an inheritance incorruptible, and undefiled, and that fadeth not away, reserved in heaven for you,"

Revelation 1:6 "And hath made us kings and priests unto God and his Father; to him be glory and dominion forever and ever. Amen."

Revelation 19:16 "And he hath on his vesture and on his thigh a name written, KING OF KINGS, AND LORD OF LORDS."

Psalm 24:7 "Lift up your heads, O ye gates; and be ye lifted up, ye everlasting doors; and the King of glory shall come in."

Psalm 24:10 "Who is the King of Glory? The Lord of hosts, he is the King of glory. Selah."

# CHAPTER 27
# A SMALL BLESSING TURNING
# INTO A BIG ONE

There is a story found in the book of John chapter 6 that shows the importance of giving the Lord what little we have and watching him multiple it beyond human comprehension. In John 6:9 we see a lad which only had five loaves and two small fishes. As the story unfolds we discover that the boy gave what he had and in verse 11 Jesus took it, blessed it, and five thousand were fed. Sometimes God expects us to give whatever we have to those around us so that He can show His power in a heavenly way.

One of my favorite songs of all time is a song entitled "Little is Much, When God Is in It." We serve an all seeing and all knowing God; that is a very present help in our time of need. The bible teaches that if we give the Lord our substance, He in return will fill our barns with blessings. Ecclesiastes 11: 1 tells us to cast our bread upon the waters and God will give it back to us in His time. His ways are not our ways, neither are His thoughts our thoughts. Our job is to listen to Christ and His job is to honor His promise. I would venture to say nearly fifty times, in my life, God has led me to give what little I had and I have watched him bless those decisions four fold. Allow me to tell you a story that is simple yet profound.

One Wednesday night, as I was getting ready for church, God clearly brought a lady to my mind and told me to give her my last five dollars. That money was intended to go into my gas tank, but I was positive

God wanted me to do this. The Lord seemed to whisper to my soul and said if you will do this I will bless you richly.

When we arrived at the house of God, that dear lady was on my heart. She had recently been saved and she was extremely faithful to the Lord. I remember shaking her hand and giving her my last five dollars. She developed a tear in her eye and I knew the Lord was in it.

After this brief exchange I took my seat and opened up the hymn book. As I was studying the song Great is Thy Faithfulness, a man slipped in behind me and took his seat. This man then suddenly grabbed me by the shoulder and dropped a hundred dollars in my lap. When this took place almost immediately the Lord spoke to my heart and said I'm a debt-or to no man. It was just by giving that lady five dollars that the Lord gave me nineteen times more then I gave out.

Please allow the Lord to take your little lunch and fed many others around you. It's a wonder why more people don't trust Christ with their little lunch, because the fact remains, He will surely reward you from His storehouse of love.

## *Scriptures Chapter 27*

John 6: 9 "There is a lad here, which hath five barley loaves, and two small fishes: but what are they among so many?"

Ecclesiastes 11:1 "Cast thy bread upon the waters: for thou shalt find after many days."

Isaiah 55:8 "For my thoughts are not your thoughts, neither are your ways my ways, saith the Lord."

# CHAPTER 28
# A WONDERFUL GIFT
# FROM GOD

Every human; young, old, rich, poor, bond or free, love to receive gifts throughout the days of their life. Romans 6:23 teaches "That the gift of God is eternal life through Jesus Christ our Lord." Often times a thoughtful gift can lift your spirit and brighten your day. James 1:17 says "That every good gift and every perfect gift cometh from above." We must give credit where credit is due when it comes to gifts that we receive.

Thankfulness is a major thing with the Lord, and we must be careful not to become cold and greedy in our life. Most people I know are so very blessed. These people have a roof over their heads, shoes on their feet, a number of cars, and toys galore. Our Great Savior has showered us with gifts untold and it is time we thank Him for what he has done.

Once in awhile things happen that humble us to the lowest degree. The Lord will move in such a gracious way, at different times, and it will literally bring us to tears. This next story is one of those types of stories. Its rarity makes it neat, and it will cheer you up and cause you to reflect on God's goodness towards us.

While I was at work one afternoon, I was asked to go on the road and pick up some signs that we had put out weeks earlier. On the way to the jobsite, I began talking to a good man and he mentioned that he had a slightly used Harley Davidson leather coat. When he mentioned that coat I knew instantly that I wanted to buy it from him for a friend of mine. Harley Davidson items are very rare and very expensive, but I was determined to buy that coat for my friend.

We started talking details and right away it was apparent to me that he didn't want to sell it. I offered him two hundred and fifty dollars, but I could tell it was special to him. After our conversation was complete that day he told me he would think it over. I then told him that I wanted to buy it for a man of God, but if he was uncomfortable please don't sell it. A few days went by and still no word on the coat.

I can remember praying that God would change his heart and allow me to buy it from him. After a few days went by, this same man approached me on a Monday morning with the coat in his hand. We talked for a minute and he said, "I don't want to sell this coat to you I would rather give it to you." He went on to say that God told him to give me the coat and he was sure of it. I asked if he was positive and he said, "Give it to that preacher friend of yours." My heart melted and I could not believe his kindness towards me. I find that hardly a day goes by without me praising the Lord for gifts like that. I believed God answered my prayer and it in turn blessed my heart.

If we took the time to reflect back on all the wonderful gifts God has sent our way, it would no doubt bless us over and over again. May we never be guilty of being unthankful for all the gifts He sends our way. He deserves all the praise for what He has done.

## Scriptures Chapter 28

Romans 6:23 "For the wages of sin is death; but the gift of God is eternal life through Jesus Christ our Lord."

James 1:17 "Every good gift and every perfect gift is from above, and cometh down from the Father of lights, with whom is no variableness neither shadow of turning."

# CHAPTER 29
# FEAR THOU NOT:
# FOR I AM WITH THEE

The benefits and blessings of being a child of God are impossible to explain. Peter had it right when he said that it is joy unspeakable and full of glory. There are thousands of promises found throughout the Bible and we will deal with a great one in this chapter.

The word of God often teaches that, the born again child of God, receives special protection from the obstacles that this world throws their way. The three Hebrew children found a fourth man in the fire. Jonah found deliverance from the belly of the whale. David said this in Psalm 18:29, "For by thee I have run through a troop; and by my God have I leaped over a wall." Isaiah declares that, "no weapon formed against thee shall prosper." The Bible teaches that God is a very present help in trouble. The Lord always promises to deliver his own when problems are looming in our life.

Isaiah 41:10 has been a favorite verse for many wonderful saints throughout the years. It reads like this, "Fear thou not; for I am with thee: be not dismayed; for I am thy God: I will strengthen thee; yea, I will help thee; yea, I will hold thee with my right hand of my righteousness." Many Giants of the Faith have rested in peace having this verse burned into their heart and mind. No matter what comes our way, this verse gives us confidence that God will be there every step of the way.

Often times in my life, sudden events have come my way that has threatened my future but God has sheltered me from all danger. Psalm

91:4 says, "He shall cover thee with his feathers and under his wings shalt thou trust: his truth shall be thy shield and buckler." More times than I could ever explain the Lord has overshadowed me with love and compassion. We find in Luke 15 the wonderful account of Christ leaving the ninety and nine and going after the one sheep in danger. The following story reminds me of that very account in the Bible.

Not long ago as I was on my way to work, the weather turned horrible and extremely slick. Living in Michigan, I found myself driving in some of the worst conditions I have ever seen. That day there were many accidents all around me; cars were in ditches, trucks were sliding into other trucks, and people had no control of their vehicles. My own personal car handles very well in the snow, but on this day I had no traction on the icy roads. My goal that morning was just to make it to work in one piece and I found even that to be a tough task.

My speed that morning never exceeded twenty miles per hour and I was nervous even being on the road. As I neared my destination, I was stopped by a red light and had major problems even stopping. When the light turned green, I recall, looking to my right and seeing a young man coming directly towards me going at around forty five miles per hour. It was to my amazement that the young man slammed on his brakes and somehow stopped his car on a dime. There was no way on earth he could have stopped in those conditions without help from God. To say it was impossible in those conditions would have been an understatement. We were both in total awe at what happened that day.

After that change of events, I arrived at work that morning and had a wonderful day. Psalm 33:8 says, "Let all the earth fear the Lord: let all the inhabitants of the world stand in awe of him." Moses said it best when he said, "Stand still and see the salvation of the Lord." When the Savior is driving the car you will have no need for an airbag. The Lord is all the protection we need.

## Scriptures Chapter 29

1 Peter 1:8 "Whom having not seen, ye love; in whom, though now ye see him not, yet believing, ye rejoice with joy unspeakable and full of glory."

Psalm 34:7 "The angel of the Lord encampeth round about them that fear him, and delivereth them."

Daniel 3:25 "He answered and said, Lo, I see four men loose, walking in the midst of the fire, and they have no hurt; and the form of the fourth is like the Son of God."

# CHAPTER 30
# JESUS IS STILL
# ALIVE AND WELL

What sets us apart, as Christians, from every other religion on earth is the fact that our God got up on resurrection morning; while other leaders lie silent in the grave. If Christ would have stayed in the tomb we would be of all men most miserable. Jesus is alive and well and his power to redeem fallen men will never change. We have complete confidence as children of God that we can boldly enter into the throne room of grace, all thanks to the blood of this risen lamb. Hebrews 13:8 declares that Jesus is the same yesterday, today and forever. The following story will highlight the fact that Jesus is still alive and well, and He is willing and able to hear your feeble cry.

Not long ago, I received glorious news that a friend of mine, Charlene Parker, wanted to take pictures with my book as she travelled through the Holy Land. When I heard this news I was speechless and humbled. All throughout the next several weeks she would send me photos she took from Israel. The pictures that she took were absolutely outstanding. Charlene had pictures from; on top of Mount Carmel, alongside the Sea of Galilee, in Bethlehem, by Mount Calvary, and of course inside the empty tomb of Jesus.

When the final day arrived for Charlene to finish her tour of Israel, she happened to be inside the empty tomb. All throughout that week we were praying for seventy two degree weather with sunshine as she took those pictures. God wonderfully granted our prayers as the weather was a perfect seventy two degrees and sunny. The pictures could not have been more beautiful, but what took place that day after I saw the pictures was even more marvelous.

Immediately after I seen the pictures I asked God to direct me to the exact verses He wanted me to read for the day. I flipped open my Bible to Luke Chapter 24:6 where it says, "He is not here but is risen." Once I read the first six verses of that chapter, a peace came over me that I could never describe and I knew God directed me to those verses. Hours later as I was arriving home, I looked and my neighbor Dan was standing in my yard just like a statue. I opened the door and Dan said to me, with much joy, "Tony guess what I read today?" I responded by saying, "What did you read," and he said, "Tony I read Luke 24 under the inspiration of the Holy Ghost." He then told me at around eleven thirty that morning God told him to read that chapter and it opened his eyes like never before. When Dan told me this news tears began to flow down my face because earlier that same morning at the same exact time God also told me to read those exact same verses. Folks only God can do something like that.

The odds of the above story happening on the same day as Charlene was in the empty tomb is nearly impossible. Thank God for Matthew 19:26 which says, "With men this is impossible but with God all things are possible." Jesus is still alive and well everyone and He is doing just fine.

## Scriptures Chapter 30

Luke 24:6 "He is not here, but is risen: remember how he spake unto you when he was yet in Galilee."

Matthew 19:26 "But Jesus beheld them, and said unto them, with men this is impossible; but with God all things are possible."

# CONCLUSION

As we conclude this project, I would personally like to thank you for taking the time to read this book. I pray that your heart was blessed and your soul was stirred with each story. As I travel through this life, I cannot help but notice just how many people live a life of defeat on a daily basis. God had never intended for us to dwell in a state of depression. John 10:10 declares, that "Christ came that we may have life, and that we might have it more abundantly." The bible has every answer to any problem life throws our way. The greatest challenge we have in life is to remain positive and happy on a constant basis no matter how bad life gets.

My reason for writing these stories is to get folks to understand that God loves them very much and He wants the best for them. The vast majority of people I will ever meet make the mistake of blaming God for the problems they face, instead of Satan. The Bible declares that the devil is a master deceiver and he is out to destroy our lives. Satan wants nothing more than for us to dwell in a state of depression all the days of our life. We must train ourselves to know that we have the victory through Christ, and we have already won the war.

One day Satan will be thrown into a lake of fire and we will dance on a street of Gold for all eternity. God shed his blood for the sins of the world, so that we could escape the flames of hell. An old song says it like this "The love of God is greater far then tongue or pen could ever tell, it goes beyond the highest star and reaches to the lowest hell." Through God's word we find that He has offered us eternal life through Jesus Christ our Lord. Hebrews 2:9 proclaims, "That he tasted death for every man." We all know John 3:16 "For God so loved the world, that he gave his only begotten Son, that whosoever believeth in him should not perish but have everlasting life." Salvation of the soul is available to all mankind, but it is up to us to receive His free gift.

John 1:12 says, "But as many as received him to them gave he power to become the sons of God, even to them that believe on his name." There will be times in all of our lives when we will feel a tug from another world. During those rare and unusual times, God will invite you to come for the saving of your soul. Although God can lead you to the Water of Life, He cannot make you drink. It is up to you to receive or reject this free gift of salvation that is offered during your lifetime.

My goal in giving you these stories is to cause you to hunger for Christ like you never have before. Romans 10:13 says, "For whosoever shall call upon the name of the Lord shall be saved." If you will seek God when He is calling you, he has promised to hear your cry for help. Like the thief on the cross, you must admit your lost condition and trust in what Christ did on the cross for the redemption of your soul. You must believe that Christ died for you, that he was buried for you, and that he rose again the third day for you according to the scriptures. The only way to gain access into heaven is to come through Christ and through Christ alone. Millions have believed the gospel through the years, and millions have found a home in glory upon death.

When you come through Christ and Christ alone you will find acceptance from a Holy God. The bible says, "When I see the blood I will pass over you." Ephesians 1:7 says, "In whom we have redemption through his blood, the forgiveness of sins." Salvation was never meant to be hard, but rather very simple." Run to Christ while you feel His spirit pleading with you and you will find peace. Please do not wait too long you may never have tomorrow. Hebrews 9:27 declares, "And as it is appointed unto men once to die and after this the judgment." Do not face God with the knowledge you have; accept His free gift today while you have a chance. May God bless you all.

## Scriptures Chapter ~ Conclusion

John 10:10 "I am come that they might have life, and that they might have it more abundantly."

Hebrews 2:9 "That he by the grace of God should taste death for every man."

John 3:16 "For God so loved the world, that he gave his only begotton Son, that whosever believeth in him should not perish, but have everlasting life."

John 1:12 "But as many as received him, to them gave he power to become the sons of God, even to them that believe on his name."

Romans 10:13 "For whosoever shall call upon the name of the Lord shall be saved."

Ephesians 1:7 "In whom we have redemption through his blood, the forgiveness of sins, according to the riches of his grace."

Hebrews 9:27 "And as it is appointed unto a man once to die, but after this the judgment."

Isaiah 55:6 "Seek ye the Lord while he may be found, call ye upon him while is near."

# Published By Parables

## OUR MISSION

The primary mission of Published By Parables, a Christian publisher, is to publish Contemporary and Classic Christian books from an evangelical perspective that honors Christ and promotes the values and virtues of His Kingdom.

## Are You An Aspiring Christian Author?

We fulfill our mission best by providing Christian authors and writers publishing options that are uniquely Christian, quick, affordable and easy to understand -- in an effort to please Christ who has called us to a writing ministry. We know the challenges of getting published, especially if you're a first-time author. God, who called you to write your book, will provide the grace sufficient to the task of getting it published.

We understand the value of a dollar; know the importance of producing a quality product; and publish what we publish for the glory of God.

Surf and Explore our site --
then use our easy-to-use "Tell Us" button
to tell us about yourself and about your book.

We're a one-stop, full-service Christian publisher.
We know our limits.  We know our capabilities.
You won't be disappointed.

www.PublishedByParables.com

PUBLISHED *by* PARABLES
*Earthly Stories with a Heavenly Meaning*